Pocket reference for veterinary statistical analysis, 3rd edition

Answers to Common Questions

Do you have a minute?

For you, yes. Yes I do. But I'm not a clinician and my last course in anything related to medicine was Mr. Robinson's high school general biology class, in 1979. I'm probably not going to understand the underpinnings of your research problem in a minute, and neither would most biostatisticians.

The underpinnings are important because something as simple as a neglecting to mention that you are including both hind limbs in a study and randomly assigning them to groups can have huge ramifications to the results.

Some questions *are* good one-minuters. The best ones are open ended and address general themes: Are dropouts a problem? Is correlation among subjects an issue? Statistical answers to general questions will lead to other, more focused questions and answers, and keep the design and analysis on course. All that, of course, takes a few minutes.

How many subjects do I need?

There are three answers to this question: (a) At least ten per group, (b) the most you can afford, and (c) the fewest number of subjects that will get at least one P<0.05.

Sample size method (c) requires sample size calculations. Methods (a) and (b) don't require sample size calculations but reviewers may want to see calculations anyway to show that the project has a hope of showing statistical significance. It's not hard to manipulate sample size calculations in sample size software by choosing a large effect size[1] (or the components of effect size) to input into the software. (Googling *sample size calculator* will show plenty of web-base sample size calculators that you can use.)

For sample size (a), 10 per group, it may be possible to convince reviewers that sample size calculations aren't needed. For a prospective,

---

[1] Effect sizes are measures of clinical effect that are not affected by sample size. There are a number of measures of effect size. A few examples examples of effect size are: a difference in group means, a difference in group means divided by a common standard deviation, and Pearson's correlation. P values are not measures of effect size because they get smaller as N gets larger. So, a P values can go from P>0.05 to P<0.05 even if there is no change in clinical effect.

small-animal studies, the reason ten is enough is based on historical evidence. There are lots of successful (where successful is defined as having at least one P<0.05) small-animal studies with ten per group. If you need more than 10 subjects per group to show statistical significance, then your effect size is going to be too small and no one will care about the results anyway.

In other words, if other researchers could get P<0.05 with n=10 per group, why can't you? Because your treatment effect is too small to care about anyway.

You can generalize the "10 per group" rule by using the same sample sizes that other, similar research has published. I done that lots of times in grant proposals, and it has never caused me problems. Be careful to use the sample size used to get the specific P<0.05, which is probably smaller than the one reported in the structured abstract or introduction where authors tend to report the pre-analysis sample size, before dropouts and exclusions.

Approach (c), the fewest number of subjects that will get at least one P<0.05, requires sample size calculations. It's *calculations* instead of *a calculation* because you will want to estimate the sample size required to get P<0.05 for several of your key outcomes and then pick the smallest (or largest, if you want all the P<0.05) of those sample sizes that should get you P<0.05 for the variable or variables

The problem with sample size calculations is that to get P<0.05 you must know things (usually averages and standard deviations) about the data before it's collected. That's why pilot studies are recommended, because those small, relatively inexpensive studies provide the ingredients necessary to calculate sample size for the primary study.

I'm not so sure that pilot studies are useful, except as a hoop to jump through for reviewers and grant agencies. It's easy to show, using simulations, that pilot data can totally *not* represent the target population. That is, the pilot data is wrong a fair bit of the time because data from a small sample size often does not represent the population.

Now, you might see a problem here. If pilot studies are often misleading, and they are misleading because they are too small to represent the data, isn't there a good chance your small study will be misleading? Yep. That's why results from so many small studies conflict with each other.

On the other hand, an advantage of a small sample size is that if P<0.05, then the effect size is probably large enough to be clinically interesting, even if it doesn't represent the population.

Finally, for multicenter studies, use one of the three sample sizes, but also have at least three subjects per group per center in the final analysis so you can assess within- and between-center variation.

What is a P value?

P values are hard to understand because they conflict with our intuition of what they should be. When researchers analyze their study, what they want to know is if their result is a real treatment effect or if the result occurred by chance. They try to assess that "real treatment effect or chance" question with P values. The problem is that the answer is not one or the other, it's a combination of both: the results are a mix of treatment effect and chance. So, a P value really only works for part of the question, and so researchers misinterpret it and use it "off label," in ways that P values aren't supposed to be used.

What researchers wish P values are, is the probability that the statistical null hypothesis[2] is

---

[2] The statistical null hypothesis is usually the opposite of the researchers' scientific hypothesis.

correct, given the data[3]. But that's not what they are. If you really want to have a crack at understanding P values, I refer you to journalist Christine Aschwanden for something readable (Google *Christine Aschwanden Not Even Scientists can Explain P-values*) and the American Statistical Association for something not so readable (Google *ASA Statement on Statistical Significance and P Values*).

Here is my crack at explaining P values. The "P" stands for probability, and a P values measures how consistent the data are with the hypotheses by answering the question, *if I had another dataset from the same experiment, what is the probability (i.e., P value) that my first dataset is more unlikely under the hypothesis than the one I have now.* So, a small P value means that the current dataset is pretty unusual under the null hypothesis, since a more extreme dataset is pretty rare. So, we would say that the hypothesis didn't generate the data.

P values are not the probability that the hypothesis is correct.

To understand P values it helps to understand how they are produced from statistical tests. Statistical tests use Aristotle's *reductio ad absurdum*

---

[3] That interpretation is a Bayesian posterior probability, not a P value

argument whereby a claim is made, and then it is shown that the claim inevitably leads to something absurd. Therefore the claim must be wrong.

For example, You've told me the Earth is flat, and I wish to prove you wrong, so I say, "But if the Earth were flat, people would fall off the edge. People do not fall off the edge of the Earth, that is absurd, therefore, the Earth cannot be flat."

Statistics modifies the *reductio* method slightly, using it to suggest a scientific hypothesis is valid by implementing the *reductio* method on the <u>opposite</u> of the scientific hypothesis.

For an example of the statistical approach to *reductio*, I wish to prove the Earth is not flat (scientific hypothesis), so I claim the opposite, that the Earth *is* flat (the opposite hypothesis, called the null hypothesis). But if the Earth were flat, people would fall off the edge. People do not fall off the edge of the Earth, that is absurd, therefore, the Earth cannot be flat. The opposite hypothesis fails, and the scientific hypothesis is accepted: the Earth is not flat.

For a biomedical example, suppose some researchers believe their new pain control therapy works better than the placebo control, so the researcher's claim (i .e., scientific hypothesis) is that the mean pain score for the treatment population will be lower than the mean pain score in the control population. Data are collected and given to the statistician.

The statistician flips the researchers' claim to the opposite: the mean pain score in the treatment population will be equal to, or greater, than the mean pain score in the control population. Then, the statistician calculates a P value *under a model that assumes the "opposite" hypothesis is true--that the new treatment is not better than placebo.*

Of course, most of the time and except for freakish bad luck, data should be consistent with the model used to generate the data (the scientific hypothesis), but now we are assuming the opposite model is the true one, the one used to generate the data. It would be absurd if the data were not consistent with the (opposite) model and we would have to accept the scientific model.

Statisticians use P values to check if data are consistent with opposite hypothesis. A small P value means that the data is not consistent with the "opposite," or statistical, hypothesis. By convention $P<0.05$ is considered an absurdly small value. That is, if $P<0.05$, then people are not falling off the earth.

Now, for our pain medication example, the statistician calculates a P value and gets $P<0.05$, which is absurd if the opposite hypothesis were true, so the opposite hypothesis did not generate the data and the scientific hypothesis probably did, and the pain therapy is statistically superior to placebo control. Note that the P value is only assessing consistency of the data to the model, not magnitude of clinical effect.

A large P value (P>0.05, for example) really means nothing. It certainly does not mean groups are equivalent. Doing a reductio ad absurdum argument and having the result not be absurd (e.g., P>0.05) does not prove anything. For example, I think the Earth is flat and people fall off the Earth! But that might mean the Earth is a pyramid shape.

If you really believe that your scientific hypothesis is true, but got P>0.05, then the P>0.05 means that your sample size was too small to control the variation in the data and your effect size was too small to detect.

What is a statistical hypothesis test?

I explained the mechanics of statistical tests in the section called "What is a P value?," but here I explain an interpretation of statistical tests. Statistical tests are simply diagnostic tests, diagnosing statistical significance, so just think of them that way.

Medical diagnostic tests take information from a subject's sample (e.g., blood or tissue) and then make inferences from that sample about the patient. A clinician doesn't really care about the sample, he or she cares about the subject, and it's well known that a subject's tissue biopsy sample (e.g., liver tissue) might not represent the real state of the organ. The clinician hopes and expects the sample is representative of the patient.

Likewise, a statistical test, like a t-test, takes information from population's sample (e.g., the animals in a study) and then makes inferences from the sample about the population of animals the sample came from. A researcher doesn't really care that a treatment worked in a sample if the results from the sample don't apply to a population.

So, statistical tests are really about populations, not samples. For example, suppose that a weight reduction pill, for moderately obese people, lowered the average weight of a treatment group 5 kg over a placebo control group, say from 100 kg to 195 kg. That's pretty good weight loss, and it's fact. The people in those groups really lost the weight and no statistical test (and no P value) is needed to see that. Those numbers are real and have nothing to do with chance or anything else.

You don't need P values to show those numbers are different, they are different.

So during conference talks, statements that suggest the P values are referring to the data are wrong. P values are statements about population parameters, not the sample. To say, "the averages are statistically different" is wrong.

But a clinician prescribing the pill to a new patient isn't prescribing it to a study participant. The clinician is prescribing it to someone in the population. Somehow the researcher has make the leap from sample to population, and that's done with a statistical test.

The statistical test tests hypotheses about populations, not samples.

Statistical tests have <u>sensitivity</u>. For medical diagnostic tests, sensitivity is the probability of correctly diagnosing a diseased subject. For statistical tests, sensitivity is the probability correctly declaring statistical significance when there is a treatment effect (on group means or whatever). Statistical sensitivity is called another name: **power**. So, power is the sensitivity of the statistical test.

Statistical tests have <u>specificity</u>. For medical diagnostic tests, specificity is the probability of correctly diagnosing a nondiseased subject. For statistical tests, specificity is the probability correctly not declaring statistical significance when there is no treatment effect. This kind of decision does not have a name in statistics.

The probability of a medical diagnostic test making a mistake by calling a diseased subject disease free is 1-sensitivity. The probability of a statistical test making the same mistake is called **type II error**. It's the probability of not declaring statistical significance (i.e., $P>0.05$) when there is a treatment effect.

The probability of a medical diagnostic test making a mistake and calling a nondiseased subject diseased is 1-specificity. The probability of a statistical test making the same mistake is called **type I error**. It's the probability of declaring statistical significance when it doesn't exist; that is, the researcher found $P<0.05$, but that is wrong, the group mean (or whatever) are really the same.

What statistical test should I use?

Statistical tests test very specific questions about populations of subjects, not the data. They test population means, medians, standard deviations, correlations, or nearly any parameter that you want to test against the same parameter from another group or against a predetermined number, like zero (correlations) or one (odds ratios).

So you simply have to pick the parameter that you want to test and then pick the corresponding test. Googling *which statistical test should I use*, and then clicking on "images," will give you decision charts detailing which statistical test to use.

Those tests will return P values come from the data, but actually address statements about the populations. So you should use a statistical test that answers a statement about the populations you are interested in.

Sometimes the populations are obvious. If 100 Labradors at an academic hospital are divided into a treatment group and a control group, then the results of the study apply to the population of Labradors those study dogs represent. That's why political pollsters work hard to get representative samples of voters for political polling so the samples reflect the population of voters.

We all understand that a study of Labradors doesn't apply to greyhounds because Labradors and greyhound populations are too different. But does a pain medication study using Labradors in New York City generalize to a population of Labradors from Ames, Iowa? Probably, but that's for you to decide.

Sometimes, the population can be hard to imagine. Suppose 20 femurs are harvested from 10 cadaver dogs from one academic hospital for a mechanical testing bone-plate strength study. A company gives the researcher 20 bone plates. Those 20 bone plates and those 20 femurs are supposed to be a representative sample of bone plates and of femurs from populations of bone plates and femurs.

"What kind of statistical test should I use?" is a common question because everyone knows that certain statistical tests are meant for certain kinds of data. There are two reasons for that:

1.   Different statistical tests test answer different questions about the populations that the data come from. For example, in a treatment versus placebo control clinical trial, a t-test would compare the means of the treatment population and control population, but a median test would compare the two populations' medians. The Levine test compares their standard deviations.

2.   Different test have different underlying assumptions that the data must satisfy in order for the test to be valid. For example, a t-test requires (a) that the observations be independent within each group (b) the observations are independent between groups, (c) both groups are normally distributed, and (d) both groups have the same standard deviations. If the data violate any of those

17

assumptions then the P value from the test will not be correct.

Almost all statistical tests have assumptions like these, and more, and they all need checking.

Researchers often check the normality assumption in a t-test, but it's very rare to read in a paper that the other assumptions have been checked. One of the most critical and common mistakes I read in veterinary manuscripts is violation of the independence assumption for t-tests or ANOVA. That most often happens when a researcher uses parts from the same animal in the same or different groups, like when 10 pairs of cadaver hind limbs from 10 dogs are split among different experimental groups. If the limbs from the same dog are in the same group, then they violate the assumption of independence within groups. If the limbs from the same dog are in two different groups then they violate the assumption of independence between groups.

Do I have too many groups?

If you have to ask, the answer is yes. I've seen dozens of studies ruined by asking too many questions and diluting the sample size. P values depend directly on sample size: N is in the denominator of the equations for P values. As N gets large, P gets small. Nearly every study can show P<0.05 with a large enough sample size per group. So, 100 subjects assigned to two groups of 50 is much more powerful than five groups of 20 each.

Do I need equal sample sizes in each group?

You don't need need the sample size in each group, but it helps the power of the statistical tests to have the same sample size. Also, if both the sample sizes are different and the standard deviations are different among the groups, the P values will be wonky.

What is a confidence interval?

A primary objective in most clinical studies is to estimate the population mean. That's usually done with the sample average, and it's called the point estimate because it's one number estimating the mean.

Another way to estimate the population mean is with a set of plausible values---that's a confidence interval. The benefit of a confidence interval is that it also describes the variation. For example, suppose that the point estimate (sample average) for weight is 80 kg. But the confidence interval gives more information; suppose it is 60 kg to 100 kg, which is usually represented as (60 kg, 100 kg). That's a 40 kg range of plausible values for the population mean, and suggests that the point estimate, 80 kg, isn't so trustworthy.

Most confidence intervals are 95% confidence intervals. That interval has the awkward interpretation that if 1000 samples were taken from the population (that is, you repeated your study 1000 times) then the population mean would be in 950 of the 1000 confidence intervals. In other words, the 95% confidence interval is wrong 5% of the time, which is consistent with using 0.05 as a cutoff for statistical significance. Statistical tests falsely declare statistical significance 5% of the time with a 0.05 cutoff.

Confidence intervals get shorter as N increases, which mean confidence intervals are

How do I randomize subjects to groups?

It's funny to see talks at conferences where researchers flip a coin to assign subjects to two groups, and they end up with the same number of subjects in each group. For two groups of 20 subjects total, the probability of flipping a coin and getting exactly 10 subjects in each group is only

0.176. So, those researchers must have done something else to get 10 per group.

Each subject in those groups has characteristics (e.g., sex, weight, genetics) that might confound their treatment outcomes, the way heavy subjects do worse than light ones in orthopedic interventions. An orthopedic study should have heavy and light subjects equally distributed across groups, not one group of heavy subjects and one group with light subjects.

The reason to randomize subjects to groups is to balance subject's confounding characteristics over the groups: the same distribution of sex, weight, genetics, and so on are in each group. If that's the case, why randomize at all, why not just look at those confounding characteristics and assign subjects to groups deterministically? Well, you can, and that's a good idea if the sample size is less than 100. Randomization is a long-run process, and expecting randomization to work for N=20 is hoping for a lot.

Just to prove the point, suppose a researcher has 20 rats, and half of them are males. The probability that randomizing balances the 10 males in two groups and puts exactly five males in each group is 0.246. That's not so good for randomization. On the other hand, if the researcher just puts males in groups without randomizing, then there will be exactly 5 males per group.

The problem is that reviewers get nervous when they don't see the word "randomized" in the method and materials section of the manuscript.

There are two approaches that can help balance measurable confounders (e.g., sex, weight) but still incorporates some randomization to help balance (maybe!) the confounders that can't be measured (e.g., some genetic factor).

The first method is called the method of minimization. In a nutshell, begin by randomizing subjects to groups. Before each subject is assigned to a group, assess how that subject will affect group balance. Put the subject in the group that needs it the most, to correct group imbalances. Google *method of minimization* to find link that explains it, and variations of it, in more detail.

The second, easier method is blocking. Begin by grouping ("blocking") subjects that are similar on measurable confounders. Those groups are called blocks. Then randomly assign subjects within each block to treatment groups from a hat (or using a list of randomly generated groups assignments). Note that blocking requires a slightly more sophisticated statistical analysis: the blocks induce a correlation among subjects. Just include a block identifier as a random effect in a mixed model. That sounds complicated, but it's not. Also note that many analysts totally ignore blocking in the analysis. Just saying.

Here is how to block randomize, using an example. Suppose there are three measurable confounders: sex, weight, and age. Convert weight into three categories (light, medium, heavy), and convert age into two categories (juvenile, adult). Now, each subject will belong to exactly one of 12 (=2x3x2) sex/weight/age blocks. A subject might be a male, light, and old.

Next take 12 sheets of paper and write the block identifier on the top of each page. The first page might be "female/light/juvenile," the second page might be "female/light/adult," the third page might be "female/medium/juvenile," and so on for the rest of the pages.

After the pages are labeled, for each page generate a sequence of group assignments. Suppose there are four treatment groups, a, b, c, and d. Page one might look like this:

female/light/juvenile
a c d b   b a d c   d a b c

Page two might look like this:

female/light/adult
a d c b b c d a a b d c

Randomizing the four treatments within groups of four prevents wonky randomizations like this one,

female/light/juvenile
a a a a a c d c d a b c

with the first five females all assigned to the same group. If only five female/light/juveniles are enrolled they will all land in treatment group "a," unbalancing the study

As each new subject is enrolled, find the subject's group assignment by turning to the page associated with the subject's block and read the group assignment off the list.

For example, the seventh female/light/juvenile enrolled

female/light/juvenile
a c d b b a d c d a b c

would be assigned to group "d."

Should I use parametric or nonparametric tests?

Statistics is one of the few fields that make formal decisions (e.g., P<0.05 is statistically significant) without complete information: Statisticians take a sample from a population and then make a conclusion about the population from the sample.

Statistician can do that by assuming things that are usually supported by the data and some pretty theory, like the outcome's population distribution underlying the data. Statisticians look at the data and then assume the population is Normally distributed, or whatever.

Some kinds of distributions are characterized by a few parameters and are members of the family called parametric distributions. For example, Normal distributions, also called Gaussian distributions, are characterized by two parameters, their mean and variance (the square of the standard deviation). A Bernoulli distribution, which describes the probability an outcome that is a single success or failure, is characterized by a single parameter: the probability of a success. Sometimes, it's just not possible to safely pick the correct distribution, like when summary measures and plots of the data look wonky and don't match any known parametric distribution. In that case, we rely on nonparametric statistics.

What makes understanding nonparametrics tricky is that nonparametrics do use parameters. The "non" in nonparametric means that the number of parameters is unknown and not fixed in advance of the analysis: the number of parameters can grow with the data. That extra flexibility accommodates data that doesn't fall into fall naturally into a parametric distribution but the cost is usually some loss of power in the nonparametric statistical test.

That's why nonparametrics are not the go-to statistical tests. If the data really are in a parametric family then a parametric test (e.g., t-test) is more powerful that a nonparametric test. On the other hand, if a parametric test is used when it shouldn't be, the P value is wrong.

A word of warning here. I commonly see researchers test for Normality using the Kolmogorov-Smirnov test. That's commendable, but it is a low-powered statistical test, which means that it's inclined to give $P > 0.05$ and suggest the data are Normally distributed. In other words, if the Kolmogorov-Smirnov test gives $P < 0.05$ you can be sure that your data are not normally distributed. But $P > 0.05$ doesn't really mean anything. As always.

There is really no harm in using a nonparametric test: it's conservative and safe. But for the conclusion section of the manuscript, make sure that you know what the nonparametric test is testing. Some of them compare population distributions, some compare medians, some compare means on ranked data. So, the groups might be different, but not in the ways that you expect or can explain easily.

For example, suppose that a researcher determines that the data are not normally distributed. Let's say the distributions are skewed. Then, the mean is may not be the best summary of the data, and t-test not the appropriate statistical test. So, the researcher runs a Wilcoxon rank sum test, gets $P < 0.05$ and claims the groups are different. That's fine, but how are the groups different? Medians? Distributions? Standard deviations?

Can I add more data after an analysis?

No, this is related to stopping early and starting again. See the next section for the particulars.

Can I terminate a study early?

No, well, yes--with the right preplanning and analyses, using interim analyses with stopping rules if you plan for them before the study starts. You can't just do analysis, like the answers and stop the study, or do the the analysis, not like the answers, and keep going.

Stopping rules is the name for the appropriate P values to used to stop a clinical trial for success or failure, or keep going, before the end of the study. The data can be checked many times—but only with the appropriate preplanning—stopping rules can't be made up on the fly.

Stopping rules can be used to stop the trial for positive results or adverse events.

The idea behind stopping rules is to have the type I error rate at 5% for the whole study, which is the same thing as doing the study without interim stops and using $P<0.05$ for statistical significance at the end of the study. If the data were checked using $P<0.05$ partway way through the study and then again at the end of the study, then the overall type I error rate would be greater than 5%. There is actually nothing wrong with doing that; it would be similar to using $P<0.1$ for statistical significance and no stopping rules.

Barring catastrophes (e.g., equipment failure), there are two reasons to stop a study before it is over: the scientific hypothesis (i.e., a medical treatment) is clearly a success, or the hypothesis is clearly a failure. One possible stopping rule is to stop the study midway through at P<0.02 (success and statistical significance) and P>0.6 (failure), but continue collecting data if the P value is between 0.02 and 0.6. If the study was not stopped, and continues to the end of the study, then statistical significance is set at P<0.03. The more times the data are checked, the smaller the level for statistical significance.

There are an infinite variety of stopping rules and Googling "clinical trials stopping rules" will give a lot of papers on the subject. Most appear to be written for statisticians, and are overly complicated for someone who just wants to use simple stopping rules. If you want to use stopping rules, the best thing is to find a statistician who had done them, or suggest that your statistician run some simple computer simulations to pick the numbers (e.g., the numbers from the previous paragraph, 0.02, 0.6).

An informative example, a parable really, is Nissen SE (2006) ADAPT: The Wrong Way to Stop a Clinical Trial. PLOS Clin Trial 1(7): e35. https://doi.org/10.1371/journal.pctr.0010035

What is inference?

Inference is the word for making a decision about population parameters based on a sample from the population.

Suppose you are at a playground and see a kid behaving rudely. If you decide the kid must have lousy parents then you are making inference about the parents based on the kid's behavior. That's statistical inference.

What is ANOVA?

ANOVA is the acronym for ANalysis Of VAriance. That name is a little confusing because ANOVA is a statistical test for the equality of more than two means, not variances. But ANOVA uses the relationships of variances to test means, and that is how it gets its name.

T-tests test the equality of two group means. ANOVA is the extension of t-tests to more than two groups.

For example, an OA pain medication trial measures pain with a continuous outcome, peak vertical force, on three treatment groups: placebo, Rimadyl, and Deramaxx. This is a standard three-arm trial.

ANOVA would test for the equality of the population means of the three groups. P<0.05 means that at least one population mean is different from the others, but doesn't state which are different, which directions they are different, or the effect size.

That's why ANOVA is always followed by pairwise t-tests, placebo versus Rimadyl, placebo versus Deramaxx, and Rimadyl versus Deramaxx, which are the comparisons we actually care about.

So why not just do the pairwise tests and skip the ANOVA? You can, as long as the P values for the pairwise tests are fixed for type I error inflation with the Bonferroni correction, Tukey's HSD, Holm's method, or any of the million other type I error inflation correction methods.

At this point you've probably read dozens of peer-reviewed published articles in which an ANOVA analysis was followed by type I error corrected pairwise tests. That's all overkill.

All you need to do is (a) ANOVA followed by uncorrected pairwise tests or (b) corrected pairwise tests without ANOVA. The reasoning for (a) is that the ANOVA is itself a way of controlling for type I error. If the ANOVA P<0.05 then you've already shown that the overall error rate is below 0.05. The reference for choosing (a) or (b) but not both is Ramsey, Fred, and Daniel Schafer. The statistical

sleuth: a course in methods of data analysis.
Cengage Learning, 2012. But I'd prefer that you
reference this book.

One advantage to (b) is that it's easier to defend
against reviewers. But (a) is usually less
conservative--your pairwise tests are more likely to
show significance.

To get correct P values from ANOVA, three
underlying assumptions must be met: (1) The
observations are independent within and between
groups, (2) the observations are normally
distributed within groups and (c) standard
deviations are equivalent across groups.

What is ANCOVA?

ANCOVA, Analysis of covariance, is just like
ANOVA except continuous outcomes can be
included and adjusted for. If there were no groups,
then ANCOVA would be regression.

For example, an OA pain medication trial measures
pain with a continuous outcome, peak vertical
force, on three treatment groups: placebo, Rimadyl,
and Deramaxx. This is a standard three-arm trial.
Unfortunately the researchers noticed that the
groups are not balanced on pretreatment weight.
The placebo group tends to the light side, and the
Deramaxx group tends to the heavy side. Putting

pretreatment weight in the ANCOVA adjusts the P value to account for the imbalance on weight.

To get correct P values from ANCOVA, three underlying assumptions must be met: (1) The observations are independent within and between groups, (2) within each group, the regression residuals[4] are normally distributed and (c) standard deviations are equivalent across groups.

What is type I error inflation and the Bonferroni correction?

In essence, the idea is to keep the overall type I error rate (the probability of a false P<0.05) at 0.05 for the entire study, or for parts of the study.

Imagine a simple clinical trial with four treatment groups and one primary outcome. Say, four different doses of a new pain med for osteoarthritis with a pain score as the outcome. To compare each group to the other groups gives six statistical tests, and those six tests are considered a family of tests. That is, they are really six parts to one inferential problem, not six different inferences. The made up one problem, and the probability of a type I error for one problem should be 0.05. But the

---

[4] Residuals are the differences between the observations and their predicted values from the regression line.

probability of a type I error from six statistical tests is a whopping 0.26, not 0.05.

Calculating lots of P values in a study may inflate the overall type I error rate, and procedures have been developed to fix that problem.

The Bonferroni correction sets a cutoff for statistical significance lower than 0.05. For example, an ANOVA with four groups has six post-hoc pairwise tests, and the Bonferroni correction is 0.05 divided by six, which is 0.0083. Now, a post-hoc test's P value must be less than 0.0083, rather than 0.05, for statistical significance.

Bonferroni works fine for a few tests, but is otherwise too conservative, cutting out results that should be statistically significant. Use the Holm-Bonferroni method when there are many more pairs of tests. Google *Holm Bonferroni* for descriptions of the method, which is easily done in spreadsheet.

Solutions to common problems

Measuring subjects more than once: Treating correlated data as independent data

Suppose I want to test the difference between men's and women's heights, and measure three men's heights and three womens' heights five times each with a good ruler within an hour timeframe. Is that N=30? Sort of, because I have recorded 30 measurements. On the other hand, not much new information is provided by the repeated measurements on the same people: I'd get pretty much the same height each time, so really there are only six pieces of information, that is, N=6.

The problem with analyzing repeated measures like they are independent is that the P value is be smaller than it should be, because the N is falsely larger than it really should be, N=30 versus N=6. So, in a manuscript, a red flag for this problem is very small P values when the number of subjects is small.

A measure that is repeated on the same subject over time (e.g., baseline, 3-month recheck, 6-month recheck) is not independent of the other measures, and can't be considered an entire new piece of information. Most researchers recognize this as a classical repeated measures problem and account for it in the analysis, often with a repeated measures ANOVA or with analysis of covariance, using the baseline as a covariate.

But repeated measure are more than repeated measurements over time, and sometimes the repeated measures sneaks into data, effectively inflating the sample size. Examples are:

- Using one limb as the treatment limb and the other as the control limb is a repeated measure. One challenging problem equine orthopedists throw at me is randomizing the four limbs from the same horse to a control group and two treatment groups. That's four limbs into three groups, so I had to account for dependence within and between groups.
- Measuring wound healing with treatment and control wounds on the same animal is a repeated measure.
- Putting different parts of the same cadaver animal into the same or different experimental groups is a repeated measure.
- Measuring dogs from the same litter or same household is may be a repeated

measure, since the dogs are related or exposed the same way.

- Measuring 100 cattle each from 5 different farms is a repeated measures problem, because the outcomes from cattle within a farm may be correlated
- Treating one joint, waiting until it heals, and then treating the same joint or contralateral joint is a repeated measure. I see that a lot with retrospective studies, when some of the same animals are included more than once because the had the same problem more than once. For example, some dogs will have bilateral stifles repaired six months apart. When the records are reviewed and retrieved, that dog is counted twice.

Beside ignoring the repeated measures, where an analysis often goes wrong is when the analysis is automatically produced with graphics, like when a correlation coefficient (and its P value) are automatically output with a scatter plot.

For example, suppose that a researcher measures vertical impulse and peak vertical force (two ground reaction forces that orthopedists measure) on each pair of hind limbs for 30 normal dogs, and plots them with a scatter plot with vertical impulse the x axis and peak vertical force on the y-axis. So far, no problem. There are 60 points on the plot, probably grouped in 30 little sets of two points, corresponding to a dog. But if the plotting software also produced a correlation coefficient, then 60 points, not 30 are going into the coefficient's P value calculation, and its P values uses N=60, not N=30. The P value for the correlation coefficient is much smaller than it should be.

Sometimes researchers want correlated data, especially when comparing a subject to its own baseline values, or measuring the trajectory of a subjects' responses over time.

There are six common ways (and lots of other, very good ways) to analyze correlated data. Not every method works for every arrangement of correlated data.

1. If the data are repeated measures over time, then simply test the groups at each time point.
2. Response feature analysis
3. Nonparametric sign test (paired data)
4. Random effects or mixed effects models
5. Repeated measures ANOVA
6. Paired t-test

Most software has repeated measure ANOVA and random effects[5] models to account for multiple measurement on the same subjects.

Measuring different parts from the same animal

See the previous section.

Calculating lots of P values (also called multiplicity)

Don't worry much about what statisticians think on this subject; among statisticians familiar with the subject, many don't agree on some fundamentals. Statisticians who haven't spent time thinking about multiplicity in the grand scheme of research are bound to follow some statistical myths and absurd conventions.

You should do what makes reviewers happy. Do Tukey's HSD or the Bonferroni correction in ANOVA situations, or the Bonferroni-Holm method when there are more than a few comparisons. For

---

[5] A random effects model simply has a term for "subject" that links each subject to all of its measurements of one outcome, like PVF. That term is called a random effect. If there are 50 dogs in a repeated measures trial, the model would have 50 random effects, one for each dog, linking the dogs to all it's measurments.

microarray analysis multiplicity corrections, seek expert help. It's not any harder, it's just that those methods have be refined over time and you should use the current standard.

The basic problem is clear: Using a cutoff of 0.05 means that each statistical test has a 5% giving a false positive result (i.e., type I error). That 5% is sort of additive with more P values, with more P values the chance of reporting a false positive result increases. For a study with 10 groups (45 pairwise comparisons) there is a 90% chance of a false positive result.

The 45 pairwise tests are called a "family" and the idea is to adjust the cutoff smaller (much less than 0.05) so that the overall "family" error rate is 5%, not 90%. Some adjustment methods for have adaptive cutoffs.

It's at this point that statisticians diverge on their approach to handling multiplicity. Some don't adjust for planned comparisons, and some do. Others prefer running an omnibus test and then not adjusting the pairwise tests.

And what about all those P values coming from testing disease risk factors instead of pairwise comparisons of groups. There isn't a formal mechanism for studying adjusting those P values.

The bottom line do what you need to do to get your paper published, but be aware that you might have some type I errors in your results.

Not interpreting P values correctly

That scream of agony you hear is me, after listening to another surgery resident claim that, because P>0.05, two groups aren't different. See the section on P values in this book while my scream echos in your ears.

Believing retrospective studies: Not interpreting study design correctly

You've noticed something about your cases over the past couple of years, a relationship between disease severity and outcomes. So, you get a student to search the case records and run a retrospective study on those cases. Lo and Behold, your hunch was correct. You have self-fulfilled your prophesy. In effect, you've looked at the data (over the last couple of years, while seeing cases), noticed a result, and then used statistics to "verify" the result.

A study reported in Bandolier looked back at all studies of transcutaneous nerve stimulation to control pain after surgery. Most of the retrospective studies reported that transcutaneous nerve stimulation controlled pain after surgery, most of the blinded, controlled randomized studies said that transcutaneous nerve stimulation did not control pain.

But see the section on confounding and bias.

Confounding and bias

The reason that retrospective studies have lower evidentiary value than prospective is because they are tangled up with bias. There are nuisance variables, like the distance the owner travels to get to the clinic, that are might affect the outcome

Calculating Post-hoc power

The problem with post-hoc power is that the number is completely unreliable. Sometimes reviewers ask authors to calculate post-hoc power, usually when there are some P>0.05 and the reviewer is concerned about type II error, that is, the sample size was too small to detect a difference in groups means.

But,
1. if P>0.05, then the sample size was too small to detect group differences. That's just a fact. Nearly

every P>0.05 can be turned into P<0.05 with a larger sample size.

2. Any number, including post-hoc power, that is calculated from data can have a confidence interval around it. Confidence intervals are a set of plausible values for power, and the confidence interval for post-hoc power is typically so wide that it makes the point estimate for power meaningless.

Sometimes, when the reviewer asks for post-hoc power, it's easier just to jump through the hoop and calculate it. But it you want to argue against it, see my letter to the editor in JAVMA and references within: Evans, Richard. "Proper use of post hoc power analyses." JAVMA 249.2 (2016): 146-146.

Randomizing small sample sizes

The primary point of randomizing subjects to treatment groups is to minimize bias. The idea is that confounding variables are balanced across groups. Confounders are those variables that you don't care about or can't measure but can affect outcomes--like the ability of a pet owner to follow instructions. Randomizing should put equal numbers of well-owned pets in all the groups. The problem is that there isn't just one confounder, but many, and having them all balanced across groups for a small sample size is impossible.

The solution is a bit tricky, because some breeds or species are more homogeneous than others. Pigs might not have to be randomized at all. Very heterogeneous species, like dogs, would need huge samples sizes to randomize properly, unless they were purpose bred laboratory dogs, which are much more like swine in terms of variation.

The solution is tricky because reviewers and others, like FDA CVM statisticians, are decades behind current statistical methodology. If you simply assign subjects to groups by hand, without randomizing, so that the group are balanced, then reviewer will likely freak out.

The best approach is to randomize subjects to groups and then check for balance on known baseline and confounding variables. If the groups are unbalanced then fix them by hand (i.e., moving subjects to other groups) but don't mention that in the paper. Hey, I'm just trying to be practical here.

This is a good overview of randomization methods, Kang, Minsoo, Brian G Ragan, and Jae-Hyeon Park. "Issues in Outcomes Research: An Overview of Randomization Techniques for Clinical Trials." Journal of Athletic Training 43.2 (2008): 215–221, and it notes the chance of imbalance when N<100.

Ascribing results to populations that are different than the sample.

Journalists and others do this all the time in human studies. A researcher reports that caffeine (or chocolate or beer) gives mice brain tumors and then the media reports that humans are going to get brain cancer from Starbucks.

I'm obviously an exaggerating, but some recognition should be made that samples from different species and different locations may not apply to other species and locations.

A more subtle problem is that doctor-to-doctor variation can be large. So while the study population of Labradors might be the same in Florida and California, the practice patterns of the study clinics are different enough to make the results possibly nontransferable.

Comparing baseline variables over groups with classical tests for mean differences

To minimize bias, researchers hope that pretreatment outcomes and nuisance variables[6] are balanced[7] across groups.

For example, a study of a drug for knee OA pain would balance subject weight, sex, body condition score and degree of OA pain over the treatment and control groups before Day 0. No researcher would want all the obese subjects in the treatment group and thin subjects in the control group, or the severely painful subjects in the treatment group and the mildly painful subjects in the controls group.

To check group balance on those variables, researchers compare the baseline variables with t-tests, Wilcoxon tests (which are nonparametric tests) or tests of proportions, depending on the kind of variable.

---

[6] Nuisance variables aren't outcomes but can affect outcomes. For example, subject body weight in an osteoarthritis pain study. The outcomes are pain measurements, but if body weight isn't balanced across groups, then the result might be the effect of body weight, not treatment.

[7] That is, have the same distribution.

There are three problems with this approach. Let's use subject weight as an example, and the researcher wants to balance subject weight across a treatment and control group, and check it with a t-test. Of course, the groups' average weights are never exactly equal. To check if that difference matters, a t-test is used. Typically, if P>0.05, the researcher would say that weight is balanced across the groups and ignore weight in the rest of the analysis.

Here are the three fatal problems:
1. If the P value from the t-test is greater than 0.05 (which is what is hoped for here), the researcher assumes that the groups are not different. That is a completely wrong interpretation of the P value. P>0.05 does not mean that the group population means are not different.

2. Statistical tests are about populations, not samples. The sample averages are surely different. Even if the population means are not different, the sample means are different and can affect inferences.

In other words, if the average weight for the treatment group is 20 kg and the average weight for the control group is 21 kg, that difference is real and can bias the results regardless of what the t-test says about the population means.

3. Statistical tests test a single parameter. Even if the statistical test is misinterpreted and the groups are assumed not different, that really means that the only one parameter (e.g., the population mean) is not different. I've seen example where the population means are considered equal, but the groups' standard deviations are wildly different due to an outlier. So one misplaced animal could wreck a study.

A better approach is to use descriptive statistics to compare the groups. Compare the effect size (for weight, for example). If effect size is greater than 0.2, then you might need to use that baseline variable as a covariate in the analysis, in an ANCOVA or regression. That sounds pesky and extra work, and it is, but not much extra work.

If you do use baseline variables as covariates, don't make the mistake of excluding them from the analysis if, in the ANCOVA, their $P > 0.05$. Only exclude covariates if they don't change the inferences for the primary outcomes. A covariate can have $P>0.05$ and still influence the model. The reason is that the P value is a statement about the population parameter, but it is the data that is influencing the model.

P-hacking

It's not hard to get at least one P<0.05 in a study by bending the rules a bit or by exploiting reviewers' statistical shortfalls, and there is a large and growing literature on the number of wrong results in the scientific literature. Simply go to Google Scholar and search "reproducibility crisis" to see a number of articles on the subject.

If you need P<0.05, or if you are reviewing a manuscript and are concerned that the authors have P hacked (bent the rules a bit), here are some things to look for:

Changing data definitions (e.g., who is diseased)

Variables with multiple levels (e.g., continuous data like weight, or scores, like lameness scores) can be transformed into new variables with different properties. For example, a 0 to 5 lameness score can be transformed into sound (0 and 1) and lame (2 to 5). So a dog that went from a 3 to a 2 is still lame, but a dog that went from a 2 to a 1 is now sound, even though both dogs changed exactly the same amount, one unit, and an analysis of "change" would show no difference in the dogs.

Subset analysis or eliminating data that "shouldn't have been included in the first place"

Try reasonable and justifiable subsets of the data until a P<0.05 shows up. Of course, you have to describe the subset in the materials and methods section, but you don't have to describe all the other subsets that were analyzed first.

Make subsets by removing subjects that shouldn't have been analyzed in the first place (e.g., animals that were too sick or not sick enough) or by analyzing specific groups of subjects classified by the outcomes.

If a field study, if P>0.05, it's not hard to look back and find subjects that should be dropped out. If the study was randomized, then once the animals are dropped out the randomization is broken and the study becomes an observational study: biases creep in, and P values less than 0.05 are ripe for the picking.

Trying different statistical analyses until one works.

This is one I'm guilty of. The statistician tries a valid analysis, but no P<0.05. So, the statistician tries another reasonable analysis, but no P<0.05. Then, the statistician tries a third reasonable analysis, and then finds a P<0.05. The final analysis is reported without mention of the first two "failed" analysis.

One reason that multiple methods are valid or appear to be valid is because statistical test or model assumptions are rarely checked and reported.

Organizations like the U.S. Food and Drug Administration Center for Veterinary Medicine try and prevent this kind of hacking by requiring investigators to prespecify their statistical models. That doesn't work, because then the investigators are often obliged to use tests and models that don't fit the data, so that the P values are wrong. No one at the FDA ever checks the statistical test and models assumptions.

Using more variables than observations

Let type I error play in your favor for a change. Using lots of variables increases the chance of a type I error (a false positive result). Type I error corrections are usually overlooked in the multiple variable situation and many corrections (Bonferroni, Tukey's HSD) were developed for post-hoc testing of pairs of groups and don't apply to multiple variables. You can tell that to a referee too.

Changing the scientific hypothesis

Did your t-test return a $P>0.05$? It probably tested the scientific hypothesis for a difference in population means. Change the scientific hypothesis to an equivalence test, a test of noninferiority, or to test a change in the direction of the results (a one sided test).

Collecting more data

If you have analyzed the data already, then adding data and re-analyzing increases type I error and increases the power, so adding data increases your chance of getting $P<0.05$. See the section called "Can I add more data after analysis."

Strong correlations

Usually it's not too hard to get a reasonably strong correlation in a prospective study. The idea is to get extreme values on the x-axis. For example, there is only a tiny correlation between height and weight in a sample of quarter horses. But if the sample includes miniature horses and draft horses, the correlation between height a weight is strong. This is also easy to do in some laboratory studies where extreme values or amounts of materials can be included in a study (e.g., dosing chickens with widely different amounts of lead to determine the correlation of lead in eggs with lead in the hens).

The right kind of statistician

One night you are driving at 100 mph down a rural Montana road, hit a cow, and end up with a brain injury. The on-call doctor in the local small town is dermatologist. Having a dermatologist treating your brain injury may be better than no treatment all, or it may not be. The dermatologist might treat your injury aggressively in the wrong direction.

Having the wrong kind of statistician analyzing your data can be worse than doing the analysis yourself.

Statisticians' specialties are more diverse and much more focused than medical professionals, and the way we label ourselves can be misleading. For example, you might think that a professor of biostatistics at a large university would be good at analyzing data, but many academic biostatisticians work on methodological problems using mathematics and analyze relatively few datasets. They leave the bulk of the data analysis to their universities' consulting centers.

My own thesis advisor considered himself an applied statistician, but he didn't know how to use any statistical software. Again, he worked on the methodological aspects relating to applied problems in survey sampling, not with the data per se.

One teaching statistician once told me, "What do you do when P>0.05, get more data?" That is absolutely and fundamentally a wrong thing to do. That person is expert at communicating statistics to undergraduates, but not at analyzing data.

Your best bet is to find a statistician who frequently analyzes biostatistical data. If you have a research program, try and cultivate the statistician by inviting him or her into the lab and to lab meetings. Make the statistician part of the team.

A template for writing the statistics section

The statistical section is the place to write like Hemingway, by using a few simple words to say what you did. I write a lot of statistics sections, and I usually write same paragraph structure. Sometimes, when researchers write the statistics section, it's the best-written part of the manuscripts because the authors aren't trying to impress their colleagues with their knowledge by using obtuse language. (Read "Jurassic Park" author, and medical doctor Michael Crichton's paper in the New England Journal of Medicine, "Medical obfuscation: structure and function." (1975): 1257-1259.)

A statistics section should have three distinct parts: (1) an introductory sentence, (2) one or two sentences listing the summary statistics and how the data distributions were checked, and (3) a list of the inferential methods (e.g., t-tests, regression), which can itself should be broken into parts by the type of analysis. If the reason for using a particular test, model, or method is not totally obvious from the context of the study design this is the place to justify your approach---in a sentence.

For example statistics section, suppose a researcher is testing a new OA analgesic against placebo in a two group (treatment and control) clinical trial. The outcomes for this example are peak vertical force (PVF) measured as a percent of body weight and a binary owner assessment of "improved" or "not improved." A real study would assess more outcomes, but this is a quick example. The outcomes were measured pretreatment at Day 0, and on Day 30, Day 60, and Day 180. Body condition scores and weight were also measured at Day 0.

This is one possible statistics section:

1. An introductory sentence giving the reader a hint of the direction of the statistical analysis. All you have to do is list, in a simple sentence, what you did.
   a. "The statistical analysis was in three parts: summary statistic calculations and data assessment, a pretreatment group comparison, and group comparisons at each time point."

2. Describe the summary statistics and data checking.
   a. "First, data summaries (scatter plots, histograms, means, medians, standard deviations, and ranges)

were used to check the data for spurious observations and outliers, and to check data distributions."[8]

3. List the statistical tests, and mention why they were used and list some of their corresponding variables.
    a. "Second, the groups were compared on baseline variables and covariates by visual inspection of histograms and by Cohen's d statistic.[9]
    b. "Third, depending on the data distributions, t-tests (PVF) or sign tests (owner assessment) were used to test differences between the treatment and control groups at each time point."

Next, suppose the same example above is changed slightly. The researchers performed a repeated measures analysis and fate has conspired to give the researchers unbalanced groups at baseline. Another possible statistics section is:

---

[8] I never use statistical tests to check for normality. Most veterinary studies don't have large enough sample size to provide the power for good inferential checks for normality.
[9] Using t-tests to check group balance on baseline variables is a common mistake. See my section in this book on checking baseline variables.

1. An introductory sentence:
   a. "The statistical analysis was in four
      parts: summary statistic calculations
      and data assessment, a
      pre-treatment group comparison to
      check for group balance, a cross
      sectional group comparison, and
      group comparisons over time."

2. List the of the summary statistics and data
   checking:
   a. "First, data summaries (scatter plots,
      histograms, means, medians,
      standard deviations, and ranges)
      were used to check the data for
      spurious observations and outliers,
      and to check data distributions."

3. List the statistical tests:
   a. "Second, the groups were compared
      on baseline measurements and
      covariates (e.g., BCS) by visual
      inspection of histograms and by
      Cohen's d statistic.
   b. "Third, depending on the data
      distributions, paired t-tests (PVF) or
      McNemar's tests (owner
      assessment) were used to test the
      difference between the treatment
      and control groups at each time
      point controlling for baseline PVF."

c. "Finally, the groups were compared over time, accounting for group differences in baseline PVF, using repeated measures ANCOVA (for PVF) or random effects logistic regression (owner assessment)."

Put together, these last paragraphs could look like,

The statistical analysis was in four parts: summary statistic calculations, a pre-treatment group comparison, and group comparisons at each time point. First, data summaries (scatter plots, histograms, means, medians, standard deviations, and ranges) were used to check the data for spurious observations and outliers, and to check data distributions. Second, the groups were compared on baseline measurements and covariates (e.g., BCS) by visual inspection of histograms and by Cohen's d statistic. Third, depending on the data distributions, paired t-tests (PVF) or McNemar's tests (owner assessment) were used to test the difference between the treatment and control groups at each time point controlling for baseline PVF. Finally, the groups were compared over time, accounting for group differences in baseline PVF, using repeated measures ANCOVA (for PVF) or random effects logistic regression (owner assessment). Statistical significance was set at P<0.05.

If you don't want to write "First," "Second," and so on, then generously use paragraph breaks. In my 120 published manuscripts, I've only had one reviewer complain about using a single sentence for a paragraph. Clearly, that reviewer has never carefully read a newspaper. Nowadays, readers prefer lots of white space on a page. White space makes a manuscript readable and the copyeditors and typesetters will change the white space if they want to, so don't worry about it.

Avoid copying statistical jargon from computer software, which often reads like an Oswald Bates lecture (Damon Wayans, https://www.youtube.com/watch?v=9ROOi5xagxg).

What this book is about

I put this section at near the end of the book because it is the least important. Statisticians get asked questions by email, over the phone, and in the hallway. It's hard to respond with formulas in those media, so we answer the questions with words but no formulas. Those explanations are enough for researchers, who are often satisfied understanding the general principles and happy to leave the formulas for the black-box statistical analysis programs. With this book,

Epilogue

In 2014, Mike Conzemius had a problem. He'd just spent several years and hundreds of thousands of research dollars searching for a couple of genes that would correlate with cruciate ligament disease in Labradors and Newfoundlands. Instead of finding a couple of important "breast cancer"-style genes that would rock the veterinary world he found a more than a dozen genes marginally correlated with knee disease—pretty much a washout in scientific terms and a huge waste of time and money.

The statistical analysis for this kind of data is more-or-less standard. Each gene is tested for group differences (disease versus not diseased), and ranked by their P values, smallest to largest. The cutoff for statistical significance is calculated by one method or another; $P < 0.05$ is too large for the number of statistical tests—the likelihood of a false-positive is too great. The actual cutoff is much, much smaller But even Mike's best gene had $p > 0.05$

At this point, most scientists would have quit and reported the results as they were. But Mike understood that statistical methods are not the Ten Commandments, not a mechanical "if this then do that," kind of reasoning and that subtle—or not so subtle—shifts is point of view could bring out considerably different answers with the same data. He also knew that generations of statistics and computer science graduate students have tinkered with nearly every possible and impossible way of looking at data. If he could think of the right question, then the answer was out there.

Instead of asking, "Which genes are correlated with knee disease," he shifted the question to, "Can I predict which dogs will get knee disease?" Geneticists prefer the first question, but clinicians and patient owners prefer the second.

His data analysis problem became a prediction problem, and there a ton of statistical prediction methods. He used a neural network method and was able to predict knee disease in those breeds with high accuracy. While each gene didn't contribute much to knee disease, a subset of genes collectively strongly influenced knee disease.

The point is that Mike didn't feel constrained by particular question, and that's not typical for medical researchers. He showed his awesome results to geneticists and they still couldn't wrap their minds around it, around shifting the problem from gene finding to disease prediction. They could only think in terms of comparing groups for each gene, one at a time and hope like hell a few genes were statistically significant.

Those skeptical geneticists have no idea what statistics is. They think it is a set of P value filters used to sort through and validate their results. Totally wrong. What it is, is, is a language.

Hemingway said, "French is the language of diplomacy. Spanish is the language of bureaucracy." And if Latin the language of medicine, then statistics is the language of reason, because researchers use statistics to reason with their peers, to convince them that the results of there relatively little dataset are real.

But all that is like saying to an English-only speaker, "If you can speak Italian, then getting a date is no problem." In desperation, the English-only speaker might memorize, *Vuoi uscire con me Venerdì sera?* (Will you go out with me Friday night?), which will work some of the time (like lots of t-tests on genetics data), but not of the prettiest girl in the room. And you want the prettiest girl in the room.

A smart English-only speaker, like Mike, knows there must be some better Italian words out there, something suave. Mike would find a native Italian speaker and ask some questions with an open mind. Then, he'd see the prettiest woman in the room and say, *Credi nell'amore a prima vista, o devo camminare da di nuovo?* (Do you believe in love at first sight, or should I walk by again?)

Don't let data wreck date night. Don't let your minimal knowledge of statistics drive your science. Find the scientific question of your dreams and then find the statistical language to answer it.